Aussie Phrases Down Under

Dianne McInnes

Published by

Pictorial Press Australia
PO Box 388, Corinda QLD 4075
Ph: 07 3716 0104
Fax: 07 3716 0105
Email: robert@pictorialpress.com.au

Reprinted 2016
Reprinted 2018

ISBN 978-1-876561-02-4

Printed by Jade Productions

Aussie Phrases Down Under

Australia's every day language is rich with slang that reflects experiences from the country's history. By borrowing Aboriginal language words and taking from convict sources, phrases developed through gold rushes, bushranging and World Wars to describe essential aspects of the Australian character and identity.

In the first 100 years of European settlement and exploration about 400 words were borrowed from some 800 Indigenous languages. Most of the borrowings were from the languages spoken in or near the major points of settlement. The words borrowed from these languages are almost exclusively nouns that refer to the external world including terms for flora, fauna, religion, ceremonies and the environment.

Between 1788 and 1852 about 150,000 convicts were transported from Britain to eastern Australia, with New South Wales and Tasmania established as penal colonies. Much of the convict language contained underworld terms, which became part of Australianism. For example, the word 'swag' has its origin in thieves' slang. It originally referred to a thief's booty or plunder. However, by the middle of the nineteenth century it was used to describe the collection of personal belongings wrapped up in a bedroll, as carried by a bush traveller. This is the beginning of the swagman tradition.

In Standard English 'muster' refers to 'an assembly of soldiers or sailors for inspection, ascertainment or verification of numbers, exercise and display'. In the Australian convict colony the term was applied to a similar assembly of convicts, and by the mid-nineteenth century it was being used to refer to the gathering together of livestock for counting and branding.

Gold was discovered in Australia in 1851, first near Bathurst in New South Wales, and then at Clunes and Buninyong in Victoria. The yellow fever, as it was commonly called, had profound social and economic effects. Some words were standard mining terminology. Some of these words came from the Californian goldfields. Many became Australianisms, but some terms lasted only as long as the gold rush period. The Australian phrase 'to knock out a living' has its origin on the goldfields, where the 'knocking out' was quite literal.

The term 'digger' in Australian myth derives from its First World War associations, but its appearance in that war owes much to the analogy drawn between the deep holes which had to be dug arduously in the search for gold, and the trenches which the soldiers had to dig. Other cultural icons from the First World War include 'ANZAC' and 'Aussie'. It was in the First World War Australian military contexts that many Australian idioms were first recorded including:

- his blood's worth bottling
- give it a burl
- hop in for one's chop
- come a gutzer
- rough as bags.

The Second World War was similarly productive of new phrases. Thousands of diggers complained humorously that they were 'goin' troppo', when they were degenerating in the tropical conditions, so this phrase found a permanent place in Australianism.

Australian English, colloquially known as 'strine' was born mainly from a mixture of the two main groups of convicts it received in its early history, The Irish and the Cockneys from East London. It is characterised by flat long vowels, speaking through the nose (but not all speakers), shortened nouns, and some consonants that are pronounced so softly they can hardly be heard.

Words with little emphasis on the consonants can easily merge into one as in the common phrase like 'Owya goin' mate?' or 'How you going mate?'

Australian English is well known for shortening nouns—surnames, place names and christian names. Generally, taking the first syllable and add a 'y' or 'o', for example Jenkins-Jenko, Woolridge-Woolly, Coolangatta-Cooly. First names with an 'r' in them will be Barry-Bazza, Sharon-Shazza and Larry-Lozza.

These days the spoken Australian English like most English languages is a mixture of the British English taught in schools and the American English more often found on the television. A colloquialism that Australians believe is central to their culture —'fair dinkum'—is borrowed from British dialect. Iconic terms such as 'the bush' and 'bushranger' have been borrowed from American English.

The special areas of Aussie creativity are in sport, in particular Aussie Rules—'boundary rider' who is the sports' reporter commenting from the side of the football field; 'desperation football' which is extremely hard-played football; 'rainmaker' that goes up into the air; 'fresh air shot' for a kick that misses; and mongrel kick for a very bad kick.

Colloquialisms sneak into politics. For example, 'dorothy dixer' is a question asked in parliament specifically to allow a propagandist reply by a minister; 'donkey vote' when a voter makes a mistake on the form so the vote is invalid; and 'free kick', which means there was an easy opportunity to score off the opposition.

Every culture has certain 'typical' behaviours—ways of standing, moving, using hands, eyes, arms and nodding the head. There are meanings associated with these movements or gestures. In Australia, it is usual to look someone in the eye when you are talking to him or her although in some cultures this may be considered impolite. Australians think that this shows directness, attention and sincerity

A significant number of Australian colloquialisms are affectionate insults or backhanded compliments. A clumsy friend or colleague may be called a 'dag', 'galah', 'drongo' or 'boofhead'. There are also many ways of saying that someone is not very useful, for example:

- couldn't find a grand piano in a one-roomed house
- couldn't blow the froth off a glass of beer
- a chop short of a Barbie
- useless as an ashtray on a motorbike.

Australianism borrows, adapts, interprets and bends from many cultures. The result is a unique Australian blend and a unique Australian point of view.

These Aussie phrases continue to grow, as demonstrated by the new 'wazza roo', which now describes dead kangaroos on the road that used to be referred to as 'road kill'.

Quintessential Australian

Mate: no other word can let you know that you're talking to an Australian than 'mate'. Even though it is used also by the Brits specifically English, and forms a great part of New Zealand speak, it is the frequency that it is used in Australia. 'Mate' is used instead of friend, or a colleague that you vaguely know or an unknown male person in your vicinity.
G'day (or Gidday) ***mate!***
Old mate—friend
Flatmate/Housemate—someone who shares a house with another person
Workmate—work colleague
Gidday! or ***G'day!***—Good day! The typical Aussie greeting
No worries mate.—This expression is based on the idea that Aussies have a laid back or relaxed attitude to life. No worries mate is used in a variety of situations: "You're welcome", "Don't you worry about it" or "I understand you".
Bloody—the great Australian superlative or intensifier. "You're bloody stupid." "Bloody hell!"

A

ABC

Australian born Chinese

A better man never stood in two shoes

A compliment!

A bit more choke and you would have started

A person has farted

A bit of an odd bod

A strange person

A bit rough round the edges

Without manners

A bit slow on the uptake

Not able to understand something

About as funny as a fart in an elevator

Not very funny

About to do her/his block

Lose control of temper

A bucket load

Large amount of something

A couple of lamingtons short of a CWA meeting

Not fully informed

Act the goat

Behave foolishly

Act your age not your shoe size

Get serious and stop being silly; grow up

Add insult to injury

Make matters worse than they already are

A face that only mothers could love

An ugly face

Air between the ears
Slow, unintelligent

All dressed up and nowhere to go
Made a mistake about time; Someone doesn't turn up

All ears
Listening attentively

All froth and no beer
Superficial; Without substance

All over him/her like a rash
Continually touches the person he/she likes

All over red rover
Completely finished

All over the place like a dog's breakfast
In a state of chaos

All piss and vinegar
Sour disposition and instigating trouble

All shine, no shoes
Fake and a fraud

All smiles
Very happy

All the go
Popular

All wool and a yard wide
Authentic; trustworthy

All your Christmases have come at once
A bonus of good luck

Alone like a country dunny
Lonely; Abandoned

Anne's your aunty
All is fine

An open slather
No hindrance to what one wishes to do

Any tick of the clock
Very soon; Any time now

A rooster one day, and a feather duster the next
Uncertainty of continued popularity or success

Arse about with care
Gone wrong because someone tried to help

As crooked as a dog's hind leg
Dishonest

As cross as a frog in a sock
Sounding angry

As happy as a worm in a can on the way home from a fishing trip
Very happy

As mean as cat's piss
Mean, stingy

As sharp as a billiard ball
Not perceptive; Mentally slow

As thick as two bricks/planks
Stupid person

At sparrow's fart
Dawn

Australian as a meat pie
Authentic

Autumn leaf
Jockey who continually falls off

Aveagoodweegend
Have fun during the weekend

Awake to something
Aware of what's going on

Away with the fairies/pixies/birds
Day dreaming

Awning over the toy shop
Man's beer belly

B

Backyard job
Illegal; Improper

Back of beyond
Away from cities and towns

Back yourself
Believe in yourself

Bad case of the trots
Diarrhoea

Baffle with bullshit
Deceive with lies

Bagman's gazette
Mythical source of bush rumours

Bag of death
Cheap red wine

Bag of doughnuts
Fat person

Bald as a bandicoot
Have no hair

Ball of muscle
Full of energy

Balls-up
Something goes wrong

Bang in the middle
Centre

Bang on the knocker
Exactly right

Barbecue stopper
Topic of conversation that is interesting/controversial

Bar flies

Old men who hang around the hotel all day

Bark at the lawn

Vomit

Barking up the wrong tree

Completely misunderstood something; totally wrong

Barmy as a bandicoot

Insane

Beat around the bush

Go around the topic; avoid the point in question

Beaten by a blow

Just beat someone at something

Beats watering the garden

About a flood

Beer goggles

When drunk, see things better than they are

Beer o'clock

End of the working day

Bee's dick

Smallest possible margin

Bee's knees

Best

Beg yours

Pardon me

Belly-up

Failure of business

Bent as a scrub tick

Dishonest; crazy; foolish

Bet like Watsons

Gamble large sums on horses

Better than a poke in the eye with a burnt stick

Not as bad as the alternative; Could be worse

Between you, me and the gatepost
Imparting important/secret information
Between the devil and the deep blue sea
Must choose between two equally unpleasant situations
Between a rock and a hard place
Making a hard decision
Blind leading the blind
Uninformed, incompetent people leading incapable people
Big bikkies
Lots of money
Big note oneself
Boasting
Billy Bluegum
Koala
Black snake it
Go to bed in work clothes
Blahdy blah blah
Etcetera; All the rest
Blood's worth bottling
Uniquely admirable qualities

Blow a fuse/your top
Lose temper
Blue flyer
Fast kangaroo
Blue-nosed wowser
Killjoy; Non-drinker; Spoils other people's fun
Blow a blue dog off the chain
Extremely windy weather
Blow shit out of someone
Reprimand someone severely
Blow your dough
Waste your money

Blow your top
Lose your temper; Become angry
Blow through
Depart hastily
Boil the billy
Put the kettle on for a cup of tea
Bog a duck in boots
Heavy mud
Boots and all
Absolutely, completely and with no reservations
Bore the pants off someone
Excessively boring person
Bottom of the harbour
Tax avoidance scheme
Box of budgies
Very bright and lively
Boys in blue
Police

Brassed off
Really annoyed/angry
Break open a coldie/tinnie
Open a beer
Brick short of a load/wall
Simple person
Bright as a two watt globe
Not a very bright person; Stupid
Bright-eyed and bushy-tailed
Happy person in good health, ready to get started
Broad in the beam
Having large hips and/or bottom
Broken packet of biscuits
Looks good on the outside, but is a mess on the inside

Brown-eyes mullet
Poo/shit floating in the sea

Buggered if I know
I have no idea

Built like a brick shit house
Someone/something strong

Bull's wool
Misleading information

Bumping ya gums
Talking too much

Bunch of fives
Punch

Bung on a blue/act
Argue; Loose temper

Bushman's clock
Kookaburra

Bust your guts
Work very hard

Busy as a blowie at a barbie
Hyperactive

Busy as a centipede on a hot plate
Very busy

Busy as a one-legged bloke in an arse kicking contest
Doing nothing

Butcher's canary
Fly; Insect

Butter wouldn't melt in your mouth
Prim, proper with a cool demeanour

BYO
Bring your own drinks/food

C

Cabbage patcher
Person from Victoria

Cack-handed
Left-handed

Call it a day
Finish up the job

Came out like a shower of shit
Very fast

Can bet London to a brick on that!
Definite

Cane toad
Person from Queensland

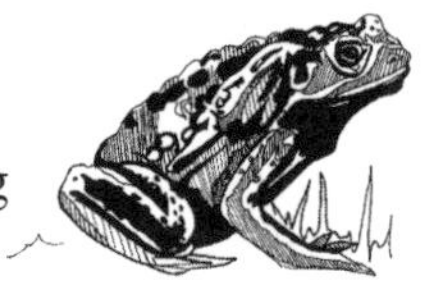

Can't handle it
Dislike/unwilling to accept something

Can't take a trick
Has a run of bad luck

Carpet grub
Small crawling child

Carry on like a pork chop
Behave in a silly manner; Frustrated/angry out of proportion

Carry the mail
Buy drinks at the pub

Cat burying shit
Very busy

Catch forty winks
Have a short sleep

Catch ya later
I will see you later

Cat's pyjamas
People who think they are better than others
Caustic crackers and strawberry sand
Have marriage and/or relationship problems
Chamber of horrors
Disgusting or horrific place
Champagne lifestyle on a beer budget
Spending more than they earn/afford
Chardonnay socialist
Derogatory label for a person who pays lip service to left-wing views while enjoying an affluent lifestyle
Charge of the light brigade
People rush in
Chateau de cardboard
Cask wine
Cheap as chips
Inexpensive
Cheque in the boot
Fired from job with no words spoken
Chew and spew
Cheap café; Takeaway food
Chewie on your boot
Aussie Rules call to incite player to miss goal
Chew someone's ear
Complain loudly; Try to cadge money
Choked up
Overwhelmed with emotion
Chop and change
Change repeatedly
Christmas on a stick
Something special
Chuck a wobbley/spaz
Throw a temper tantrum; Very upset

Chuck it in
Quit
Clagged out the bag
Worn out; Exhausted
Climb the wall
Go mad
Clued up
Well informed
Clumsy as a duck in a ploughed paddock
Very clumsy; Crude
Cock and bull story
Lie; Unbelieveable story
Cockatoo weather
Fine by day, rain at night
Cocky's joy
Golden syrup
Cocky on the biscuit tin
On the outside looking in

Cockroach
Person from New South Wales
Cold and dark as a bushman's grave
Very cold and gloomy
Cold as a mother-in-law's kiss
Cold weather; Unwelcoming
Cold as a witch's tit
Very cold
Colonial oath
Emphatic agreement
Come a clanger
Make an embarrassing mistake
Come a cropper
Fall over

Come a gutser
Make a mistake; Have an accident
Come on slow coach!
Lagging behind; Slow; Lazy
Come the raw prawn
Pretend to be naïve
Con job
Duping/swindling someone
Cook the books
Fiddle with the accounts in a business; Falsify the figures
Cop a piece of lead
Be hit by a bullet
Cop it sweet
Get what is coming to you
Cop shop
Police station
Cop this, young 'Arry
Said before punching someone
Could eat a horse and chase the rider/jockey
Very hungry
Could eat a pineapple through a tennis racket
Big front teeth that stick out
Could kick the arse off an emu
Very good health
Could eat the crutch out of a low-flying duck
Describing hunger
Couldn't be done in a month of Sundays
Take a long time
Couldn't drive ducks to water
Hopeless car driver
Couldn't drive a nail into a bucket of water
Having trouble inserting one object inside another

Couldn't fart in a bottle

Utterly useless

Couldn't fight his way out of a paper bag

Weak; Inept

Couldn't find his buttocks with both hands, a roadmap and a flashlight

Acting stupid

Couldn't get a kick in a stampede/cow yard

Poorly performing football player

Couldn't give a continental

Lack of concern

Couldn't give away cheese at a rats' picnic

Utterly hopeless

Couldn't give a shit

Do not care

Couldn't hit the side of a barn

Poor aim

Couldn't organise a fart in a bean factory

Stupid; Inept

Couldn't pull the skin off a custard

Weak; Can't throw (sport)

Couldn't run a bath

Hopeless at organising/running a business

Couldn't run a chook raffle in a country pub

Thoroughly incompetent; No organisational skills

Couldn't win if he started the night before

Slow racehorse/person

Could sell boomerangs to the Aboriginals

Very persuasive

Could talk the leg off a horse

Talks too much

Could talk under wet cement

Talks too much

Couple of pies short of a grand final
Stupid
Cow cocky
Dairy farmer
Cow juice
Milk from a cow
Crack onto...
Pursue someone romantically
Crash hat
First rate; Excellent
Croak it
Die
Crooked as a dog's hind leg
Devious, dishonest individual
Crow-eater
Person from South Australia
Crumb gatherer
AFL player who is good at getting the ball
Cry over spilt milk
Do not be upset about making a mistake that you cannot fix
Cultural cringe
National inferiority complex regarding Australian artistic accomplishments when compared to the rest of the world
Cunning as a dunny rat
Very sly
Cup of tea, a Bex and a good like down
Cure-all; The remedy for any problem
Curiosity killed the cat
Inquisitiveness leads to dangerous situations
Curry favour
Attempting to gain favour or ingratiate oneself by officious courtesy/flattery

Cut lunch commando
Army reservist
Cut off your nose to spite your face
Needlessly self-destructive over-reaction to a problem
Cuts me up
Makes me laugh

D

Dab hand at it

Skilled

Dangle the Dunlops (tyres)

Lower the wheels of an aircraft

Darling shower

Dust storm

Darwin pyjamas

No pyjamas

Dead as a maggot

State of undeniable lifelessness

Dead as mutton chops

Dead

Dead but won't lie down

Persistent person

Dead cert

Sure thing/certainty, especially in horse racing

Dead sinker

Long glass of beer

Dead to the world

In a deep sleep

Deaf as a doorpost

Unable to hear at all

Deep pockets

Person with a lot of money, but does not use it

Delicate as a starved dingo

Appalling table manners

Didn't bat an eyelid

No emotion/reaction

Didn't come down in the last shower
Shrewd; Quick witted
Died in the arse
Failed miserably
Dig a hole and bury me, it doesn't get any better than this
Happy and contented
Dingoes must have been here
Food all over the table
Do a flit
Run away; Escape responsibility
Do a Melba
Continually return from retirement
Do a perish
Die
Do your lolly
Shouting in an angry way
Doesn't give a bugger
Does not care
Doesn't know if he/she's Arthur or Martha
Confused
Doesn't miss a trick
Alert to every opportunity
Dogs are barking
Hot racing horse
Doing a roaring trade
Doing well in business
Do me a favour
Do not tell lies
Donkey's years
Very long time
Don't come the raw prawn with me
Do not treat me like a fool

Don't do anything I wouldn't do
Joking advice to someone going away

Don't fret your freckle
Do not worry/stress

Don't get off your bike
Calm down

Don't give a hang
Not worried; Don't care

Don't pick your nose or your head will cave in
Contemptuous advice to a person

Don't piss on my back and tell me that it's raining
Someone who betrays/cheats/lies to you

Don't stick yer bib in
Do not interfere

Don't strain yourself
Not helping with the task

Do the dirty on
Cheat/betray someone

Do the trick
Carry out a robbery; Will work

Do your block/nut/lolly/na-na
Lose your temper; Throw a tantrum

Do your dash
Reach one's limit, especially with regard to gambling

Dorothy dixer
Pre-arranged question in parliament

Down the drain
For the worse

Down to the last crust
Only a little money left

Down the gurgler
Something is lost

Dragin' your feet

Doing something slowly because you do not want to do it

Draw the crabs

Attracts unwelcome attention

Dreadful lurgy

Infectious illness, usually the cold or flu

Dribs and drabs

Bit by bit

Drink with the flies

Drink alone

Drive the porcelain bus

Vomit into the toilet bowl

Drives uphill with the clutch slipping

Stupid individual

Drop a clanger

Say something inappropriate

Drop in a bucket/ocean

Small/unimportant amount

Drop kick

Stupid, worthless person

Drop one's lunch

Fart

Drop your bundle

Lose control; Have a nervous breakdown

Drop your guts

Fart loudly

Drown some worms

Go fishing

Drunk as a skunk

Very drunk

Dry as a dead dingo's donger

Very thirsty

Dry as an old lady's talcum powder/pommies bath mat
In desperate need of an alcoholic drink

Duck's dinner
Drinking with nothing to eat

Duck's disease
Having a long body and short legs

Ducks on the pond
Look out, females approaching

Dull as dishwater/month of Sundays
Boring person

E

Easy as pushing shit uphill with a toothpick
Extremely difficult if not impossible

Easy as spearing an eel with a spoon
Extremely difficult

Eight, ten, two, and a quarter
Balanced diet

Engine's conked out
Engine is broken down

Enough bends to break a snake's back
Bending, twisting, winding road

Even blind Freddy could see that
Obvious

Every man and his dog
Crowds of people

Everything, but the kitchen sink
Lots of different things that are usually not needed

Everything's rosy
All is going well

Eyes off, hands off
Okay to look, but not okay to touch

F

Face like a chook's arse

A miserable expression

Face like a festered pickle

Acne

Fandangled thing

Frustrating contraption that is hard to operate

Fantasamagorical

Wonderful, amazing item/event

Feeding time at the zoo

People rushing, especially at food buffets

Feed the chooks

Give information to a group of journal

Feeling a bit peckish

Hungry

Feeling pretty snaky today

In a bad mood

Fell on deaf ears

Ignored by the person they were talking to

Few stubbies short of a six pack

Lacking in intelligence

Fight dirty

Use unfair tactics

Find your feet

Become familiar with and confident in a new situation

Fit as a fiddle

Healthy and well

Five finger discount

Shoplifting

Flappin your gums
Talk about topics that you do not understand and know

Flash as a rat with a gold tooth
Well groomed

Flat out like a lizard drinking
Working extremely hard; Very busy

Flat to the boards
Extremely busy

Flip your lid
Get angry

Floating on ice
Drunk

Flog the cat
Indulge in self pity

Flying the Aussie flag
Person out in public with shirt untucked

For crying out loud
Expression of annoyance

For fun and fancy to please old Nancy
Sarcastic answer to: 'What are you doing?'

Four wheels in the city
Top-of-the-line four-wheel drive vehicles that do not go off the road

Frig around
Behave stupidly; Waste time

From a mile off
Obvious

From go to woe
Start to finish

From arsehole to breakfast time
Long distance; Covered from head to toe in dirt

From barrier to box
Horse led from start to finish

From the get go
From the beginning

Froth and bubble
Not much substance

Full as a fat woman's underwear
Drunk

Full as a seaside dunny on Boxing Day
Eaten and drunk too much alcohol and food

Full as a state school
Bloated from eating too much

Full of beans
Energetic

Full of it
A person who talks nonsense; Conceited person

Full up to dolly's wax/pussy's bow
Have eaten enough/too much

Funny as a fart in a phone box/elevator
Not amusing

Further back than Walla Walla
Way behind schedule; Last by a long way

G

Galah session
Radio talkback session

Game's up
Caught in the act of an illegal activity

G'day, how ya goin?
Hello, how are you?

Get a life
You devote an inordinate amount of time to trivial or hopeless matters (taunt)

Get a load of...
Have a look at...

Get away with murder
Do something wrong and not be punished

Get nowhere fast
Make no progress

Get off your bike
Lose control of your temper

Get off your high horse
Stop behaving in a haughty, self-righteous manner

Get on like a house on fire
Friendship; Enjoy each other's company

Get on your bike
Go away

Get on your goat
Irritate; Annoy

Get real
Behave like you are in the real world

Get rinsed
Get drunk

Get the axe
Lose your job
Get the drift
Do you understand/comprehend
Get the giddy up
Let's go; Hurry up
Get the Guernsey
Receive an award/recognition
Get your arse into gear
Hurry up; Get organised
Give 'er a bell
Telephone someone
Give him/her the flick
Get rid of a boy/girl friend
Give it a whirl/burl
Attempt to do something

Give it the once over
Check something out
Give someone a bit of curry
Assault someone verbally/physically
Give someone the boot
Fire someone from their job; End a relationship
Give someone the irrits
Annoy/irritate someone
Give someone the rounds of the table/kitchen
Give someone a severe lecture
Give someone the willies
Create tension or uneasiness
Give us a durry mate?
Can I have a cigarette?
Give us a gander?
Can I look?
Glass of squashed grapes
Glass of wine

Glutton for punishment

Does not know when to quit

Go crook

Get angry

Go down the gurgler

To fail in a business venture/enterprise

Go fly a kite

Go away

Go for a bo-peep

Take a sly look at something that is not your business

Go for the doctor

Take action

Go hammer and tongs

Work fast; Fight

Go home to the ball and chain

Go home to the wife

Going at it like rabbits

Does not procrastinate; Does it now and finishes it

Going like hot cakes

Selling fast

Going off like a frog in a sock

Going crazy; Angry

Going ten to the dozen

Working fast

Going there and back to see how far it is

Answer to: 'Where are you going?' when you do not want to reveal where you are going

Going to see a man about a dog

Urinate; Go somewhere without revealing exactly where

Going to see a star about a twinkle

Going to the toilet

Going to throw on the nose-bag

Eat food

Going to tub up
Take a bath

Go like hot cakes
Sell easily and quickly

Go off the rails
Spoiled by bad management

Gone on...
To be in love with...

Gone thru like a dose of salts
Hurrying and doing things quickly; Busy and active

Gone to the dogs
No longer good

Gone troppo
Go crazy after living too long in the tropical north

Go off half-cocked
Rush into something without thinking

Got a head on him like a robber's dog
Ugly

Got me!
I don't know!

Got more balls than Keno
Showing determination

Go to town
Berate someone

Got punters' eyes
Think can win at gambling; Cross-eyed

Got space to rent/sell between the ears
Brainless; Stupid

Got the game by the throat
In control of a situation

Got tickets on yourself
Think very highly of self

Go through like a dose of salts
Work very fast; Diarrhoea

Go two rounds with a revolving door

Weak/ineffectual person

Got you by the short and curlies

Trapped by an opponent and cannot escape easily

Grab by the balls

Influence/impress someone

Grasping/clutching at straws

Trying to find some way to succeed when nothing works

Graveyard chompers

False teeth

Grey ghost

Parking inspector

Grey nomad

Senior citizen living the caravan/campervan way of life

Grinning like a shot fox

Very happy; Smugly satisfied

Grizzle guts

A complainer

Grog shop

Place that sells alcohol

Grumble bum

A complainer

Gumsucker

Person from Victoria

Gun it

Go fast

Guy thing

Something that only men understand and want to do

H

Had the bean
Broken
Hair like a bush pig's arse
Unmanageable hair
Ham and beef shop
Delicatessen
Handles like a dog on lino
Does not work properly
Hang out for
Wait with much anticipation
Hang the expense
Never mind what it costs
Happy as a box full of birds
In high spirits
Happy as a boxing kangaroo in a log
Very miserable
Happy as a pig on Father's Day
Depressed; Miserable
Happy as a boxing kangaroo in a fog
Very miserable
Hard/stiff cheese mate
Bad luck
Has a death adder in his/her pocket
Mean person who will not spend money
Has a few palings missing from the fence
Simple; Mentally unstable
Has a Japanese bladder
Urinates frequently

Has a snout on (someone)
Holds a grudge

Hasn't got a bean/cracker
No money

Hasn't got all four paws on the mouse
Slow witted

Hasn't got an earthly
Has no chance/idea

Hasn't got two bob to rub together
Has no money

Has white ants in the woodwork
Mentally unbalanced

Have a barney
Fight; Argument

Have a lash at it
Make an attempt at a task

Have a lend of
Take advantage of someone

Have a sticky-beak
Being nosy

Haven't they fed the dingoes lately
Greeting to an unexpected guest

Have to run around in the shower to get wet
Very thin person

Having a bludge
Lazy; Does not work

Having a perve
Looking lustfully at the opposite sex

Having a shocker
Situation is bad

Head like a busted sofa
Wild/unruly hair

Head like a half-sucked mango and a body like a burst sausage
Unattractive person
Head like a mini with the doors open
Have large/protruding ears
Hedge your bets
Avoid committing; Have a way to retreat/get away
Hells bells and bootlaces!
Hey! That's a surprise!
Here's looking at you sideways!
Thank you, and a toast before drinking
Here's mud in your eye
Pleasant toast before drinking
He's a cocky
A farmer
He's tinny
Lucky
He's true blue
The real thing; Trustworthy
Hey, Hell and Booligal
Long, long way away
High as a dingo's howl
Something smells
Hinges on…
All depends on…
Hip pocket nerve
Government increases the cost of living
Hit the road
Begin a journey; Leave the premises
Hit the ground running
Immediately work hard and successfully at a new activity
Hold those brumbies back big fella
Calm down

Hold your horses

Wait awhile

Hole in the wall

Automatic teller machine (ATM)

Holus-bolus

All of it; All at once

Hot under the collar

Get angry

How long is a piece of string?

Answer to an unknown/unpredictable question

How's it hanging?

How is everything going?

How ya travellin?

How are you?

How's your mother's chooks?

How are you?

How ya goin' mate, orright?

How are you mate? All right?

I

If his brain was electricity, he would be a walkin blackout
Stupid person

If I bought a kangaroo, it wouldn't hop
Unlucky

If it was raining custard, I'd only have a fork
Very unlucky

If it was raining palaces, I'd get hit by the dunny door
Very unlucky

If I've told you once, I've told you a thousand times
Scolding someone; Exasperation

If you can't run with the big dogs, don't get off the verandah
If you are getting stressed, choose an alternative course of action

I hope your chooks turn into emus and kick your dunny down
Common Australian curse

I'll be a monkey's uncle
Expression of surprise/amazement

I'll have your blood for breakfast
You are in trouble

I'll have your guts for garters
I will punish you

I'll pay that
Acknowledgement that one has been outsmarted

I'm buggered, broke and bewildered
Tired, underpaid and overworked

I'm easy
I do not care; It is all the same to me

In a tizz
Very confused

In cahoots with…

In partnership with... (often suggesting illegal activities)

In more shit than Ned Kelly

In trouble

I'm not pissing in your pocket mate

I am telling the truth

In the altogether/nuddy

Naked

In the nick

In prison

In the tin

In trouble

In two shakes of a duck's/lamb's tail

Short time

It can't get any better than this

Happy and enjoying life

It couldn't be done in a month of Sundays

It will take a long time

It must be rough on the bay

Seeing a flock of seagulls in the city

It runs on the smell of an oily rag

An economical car

It's a freckle past a hair

Humourous answer to: 'What time is it?'

It's cactus

Broken; Does not work

It's a take

Deceptive situation; Fraud

It's a wigwam for a goose's bridle

Answer to: 'What is it?' (mind your own business)

It's gone walkabout

Lost it

It's just not cricket

Not the right thing to do

It's not worth a brass razoo

Worthless

It was so wet even the mirages overflowed

Flood

I've been to Manly/Stradbroke

Humourous answer to: 'Have you been overseas?'

I've had it

Extreme frustration

It's within cooee of here

Nearby

J

Jack in the box

Someone who cannot sit still

Jack of something

Sick and tired of something

Jumped up

Conceited

Jump the rattler

Catch an illegal ride on train

Just around the corner

Nearby; Soon

Just let me wet me whistle

Need a drink

Just quietly

Do not tell anyone

K

Kangaroos loose in the top paddock
Crazy

Kath-and-Kim-speak
Words from Kath and Kim television series

Keep one for Ron
Keep something in reserve for the future

Keep your ear to the ground
Listen carefully and attentively; Stay informed

Keep your pecker up
Be cheerful/positive

Keg on legs
Big drinker

Kettle of fish
Difficult situation; Problem

King cobra
Go to bed in dirty work clothes

Kite flyer
Person passing bad cheques

Knickers in a knot
Upset

Knock 'em down
Violent thunderstorm in the Northern Territory

Knock it on the head
Put a stop to it

Know a thing or two
Knowledgeable

L

Last about as long as a snowflake in summer
Only works for a short time
Lead you up the garden path
Give you the wrong information
Leave for dead
Overtake; Out-perform
Leave you short
Not have enough money
Left in the lurch
Abandoned in a time of need
Left out in the cold
Not informed
Left, right and centre
Searching all around the place
Let one go
Fart

Lickety spit
Quick wash
Lickety split
Leave quickly
Lick you to death
Not a protective dog/bodyguard
Lift doesn't go all the way to the top floor
Mentally deficient
Lights are on but nobody's home
Stupid person
Like a blue-arsed fly
Disorganised

Like a chook with its head cut off
Frustrated; Erratic
Like a cut snake
Extremely agitated
Like a fart in a bottle
Agitated
Like flies around a cow yard
People wanting a free drink
Like a pickpocket at a nudists' camp
Confused; Uncomfortable
Like a pimple on a pumpkin
Very obvious
Like a possum in a gum tree
Very comfortable/happy
Like a rat up a drainpipe/rope
Very quickly
Like a stunned mullet
Dazed and confused
Like a ton of bricks
With great force

Like a two-bob watch
Unreliable; Cheap; Making a fuss
Like an old maid's pram
Empty
Like to be a fly on the wall
Be there secretly seeing and hearing what happens
Like two ferrets fighting in a sack
A woman's large wobbly backside
Like watching paint dry
A boring event
Life wasn't meant to be easy
A person is supposed to work for a living

Like a school at Christmas
Has no class
Like putting Dracula in charge of a blood bank
Unwise decision
Liquid sunshine
Rain
Lit up like a Manly ferry
Drunk
Little on the nose
Smelly
Lively as a blowfly on a winter's day
Lethargic
Living the life of Riley
Living a carefree, luxurious life
Live on the smell of an oily rag
Survive on minimum food and income
Lob on over
Go to a place

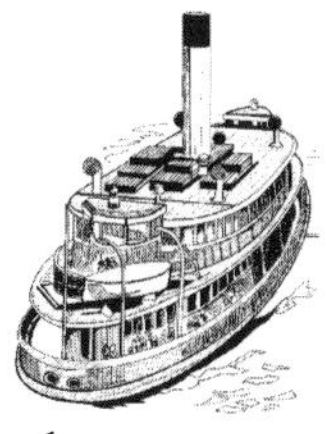

Lollipop lady/man
Person supervising road crossing near school
Lolly water
Drink without alcohol
London to a brick
Betting large odds; Absolute certainty
Long in the tooth
Old
Long streak of misery
Very tall person; Arrogant person
Long time no see
Have not seen someone for a really long time
Looks like an unmade bed
Untidily dressed

Looks like death warmed up
Looks very ill

Looks like something the cat dragged in
Untidy and dirty

Looks like something the chooks have been scratching in
Untidy, dirty place

Looks like the wild man from Borneo
Untidy man

Lord it over (someone)
Gloat about something

Lord or Lady Muck
Snobbish person

Lost me
I cannot understand what is being said

Love to stay and count our brain cells one by one, but we can't
We have no time

Lower than a snake's belly
Dishonest and untrustworthy

M

Make a blue
Make a mistake
Make a botch of it
Mess it up
Make a custard out of...
Beat someone either in a fight or contest
Make a production of...
Over-fussy
Make a proper galah of…
Make a complete fool of…
Make feathers fly
Cause a commotion
Make like a tree and leave
Go away
Make mince meat out of...
Physically or verbally attack...
Make sheep eyes at...
Adoring looks at...
Mean as bird shit
Tight fisted with money
Mickey Mouse
Wonderful; Excellent
Middle of nowhere
In the outback
Miserable as a bandicoot
Extremely unhappy
Misery guts
Unhappy person

Molly dooker
Left-handed

Month of Sundays
Very long time

Moo juice and cow cordial
Full cream milk and low fat milk

More arse than class
More luck than style

More corrugation than a water tank
Rolls of fat

More front than Myers/David Jones
Exceptionally cheeky self-assured person

More movements than a Swiss watch
Devious/untrustworthy person

Mousetraps in his pockets
Miserly individual who will not spend money

Mouthful of marbles
Posh snobby speech; Incoherent speech

Mucking around
Acting the fool; Wasting time

Mulga madness
Going crazy after living too long in the bush

My stomach thinks my throat's cut
I am very hungry

N

Nasty end of woop woop

Place a long long way

Nasty piece of work

Unpleasant person

Need a cut lunch and a waterbag

Answer to: 'Is it far, mate?' if it is a long way

Nervous as a long-tailed cat in a room full of rocking chairs

Extremely nervous

Next to the marble orchard

Next to the cemetery

No bloody picnic

A total disaster; Difficult situation

Nose-bleed seats

Cheap seats, far back and high up

Nose down, bum up

Hard at work

Not all there

Simple person

Not a patch on...

Nowhere near as good as...

Not an earthly

No chance at all

Not a sausage

Nothing

Not backward in coming forward

Brash rude person

Not fussed

Not worried about what alternative is chosen

Not give a toss

Do not care

Not made of wood and water

Cannot do everything at once

Not my cup of tea

Not to my liking

Not the full quid/packet of bickies

Stupid person

Not the sharpest knife in the cutlery drawer

Slow thinking person

Not the sharpest tool in the shed

Slow thinking person

Not what it's cracked up to be

Disappointing

Not within a bull's roar

Not anywhere near

Not within a cooee

Not within hearing distance

Not within a cooee of finishing that job

It will be a long time before the work is completed

No worries

Not a problem, I can do it

Nudge the turps

Drink alcohol to excess

O

Off like a bucket of prawns in the sun
Departs hastily

Off one's face
Drunk; Affected by drugs

Off one's trolley
Insane; Irrational; Crazy

Off the beaten track
Uncommon; Out of the way

Off to the bog to leave an offering
Go to the toilet

Off your trolley
Gone mad/crazy

Off your tucker
Not hungry

Oi! Hey you!
What do you think you are doing?

Old one-two
Violence; Fighting

On a high
In a state of happiness

On the ball
Ready for anything

On the outer
Rejected by others

On the turps
Drinking too much alcohol

On the wagon
Not drinking alcohol

On the wallaby
Travelling through the country
On the wrong track
An incorrect train of thought
Once over
Inspect something
One foot in the grave and the other on a banana skin
Live in a dangerous way and not care
One for justin
Just in case
One up against your duckhouse
Setback
On for young and old
Commotion; Fight; Argument
On the bones of one's bum
Financially ruined
On the receiving end
Receiver of something unpleasant; Loosing when boxing
On the square with
Dealing honestly with someone
On the tin roof
Provided free of charge by the management
On the turps
Drinking alcohol to excess
On the wagon
Not drinking alcohol
On ya mate!
Well done!
Open and shut case
Obvious
Open slather
No restraints

Order of the boot
Fired from job
Out in the back blocks/sticks
Beyond suburbia; Rural property
Out of the box
Exceptionally good
Out of circulation
Social recluse
Out of whack
Disorderly
Over a barrel
At a disadvantage
Over my dead body
Will not let something happen
Owner operator
Independently owned

P

Pack a wallop

Having a strong impact; Powerful

Pack of bludgers

Contempt for a group of people

Pack of poo tickets

Toilet paper

Packing polenta

Extremely scared

Pack of galahs

Group of disliked people

Paddock bomb

Old car used to drive off-road around the farm

Paper Aussie

Naturalised Australian citizen

Park a tiger on the rug

Vomit

Pass over the Great Divide

Die

Pay though the nose

Spend too much cash; Pay more than it is worth

Pea brain

Not very smart person

Piccaninny Dawn

Just before it gets light and the sun rises

Piece of cake

Easy

Pick/pull the skin off a rice-pudding

Weak/ineffectual person

Pig-headed
Stubborn
Pipped at the post
Narrowly lose
Piss and wind
No substance
Piss in my pocket/same pot
Act ingratiatingly
Piss into the wind
Do something against the odds
Piss it in
Win easily
Pitt/Collins Street farmer
Using country property losses for city/tax advantages
Plant the foot
Drive fast
Play funny buggers
Behave stupidly; To cheat
Play possum
Pretend to do something; Pretend to be asleep
Point the bone at
Blame someone for something
Popular as a mangy dog
Not popular
Pot calling the kettle black
Saying something bad about someone that also applies to you
Professional ratbag
Not to be trusted conman
Pull a swifty
Deceive someone
Pulling up stumps
Moving from one house to another

Pull someone's leg
Play a joke

Pull the wool over your eyes
To deceive

Pull up your socks
Improve your performance

Pull your finger out
Hurry up and get it done

Pull your head in mate
Mind your own business

Pull your lip over your head and swallow
Go away; Shut up

Punch the bundy
Check into work at the appointed time

Purple patch
Run of bad luck

You're pulling my leg!
(You're joking!)

Push up zeds
Have a sleep

Pussyfoot around
Trying too hard not to offend

Put a cork/sock in it
Shut up

Put a smile on your face
Make you happy

Put hairs on ya chest
Something scary; Drink/eat something strong/hot

Put that in your pipe and smoke it
Gloating insult

Put the bite on
Ask/pressure someone for money

Put the boot in
Attack someone when they are down

Put the wind up

Urging/frightening someone into doing something

Put things on hold

Postpone something

Put up job

A deceptive way of doing something

Put up or shut up

Show you can do it or be quiet

Quick as a wombat on a lazy day

Dim-witted person

Quit harping

Stop nagging

R

Rats of the air
Pigeons
Rats on stilts
Greyhounds
Rearrange someone's face
Beat someone up
Receive the order of the boot
Get fired
Reds under the bed
Being afraid; Looking for things that are not there
Right up your alley
It would be perfect for you
Roaming around like a lost sheep
Wander aimlessly; Lost
Roar the tripe out of
Verbally abuse
Rocking horse shit
Extremely hard to find
Room in a railway station
Poor person
Rough as bags/a pig's breakfast
Uncouth, unpleasant appearance
Rough end of the pineapple/stick
Hostile/unfair treatment
Rubber cheque
No money in bank account
Run about like a chook with its head cut off
Hurry around pointlessly

Run like a hairy goat
Rush about ineffectively; Run poorly in a horse race

Run like stink
Run fast

Run in with someone
Disagreement

Run of outs
Losing streak

Run rings around it/him/her
Much better

Run the rabbit
Obtain alcohol after hours

Rush your fences
Act without thinking

S

Sandwich short of a picnic
Unintelligent
Say it, don't spray it
Do not spit when you talk
Scarce as rocking horse shit/hen's teeth
Rare
Screaming heebie jeebies
Terror; Frightening
See a man about a dog
Go to the toilet
Seen better heads on a glass of beer
Ugly person

Seen the last gum tree
Die
Sell ice to the Eskimos
Ability to sell anything to anyone
Selling tickets on him/her self
Conceited
Settle petal
Relax; Do not get uptight/upset
Seven-course meal
Six-pack of beer and a meat pie
See ya on the flip side
Talk to you later
Shadow of his former self
Less strong and powerful than you were in the past
Shake hands with the wife's best friend
Male urinating

Shake someone down
Rob someone
Shaping up a beaut
Doing well; Almost finished
She'll be apples
Everything will be all right
She's sweet
Everything is fine, don't worry
Shit bricks
Very scared
Shit for brains
Stupid
Shit it in
Win easily
Shit stinks, eggs don't bounce, and you can't buy generals in a general store
Humourous answer to: 'What do you know?'

Shoot a fairy/duck
Fart
Shoot through like a Bondi tram
Make a hasty departure
Short arms and deep pockets
Has money, but will not share/spend it
Short of numbers in the Upper House
Stupid
Showing more than a Roman sandal
Showing plenty of guts
Show you the ropes
Teach someone how to do something
Shut your trap/north and south!
Be quiet!
Sick as a dog
Very ill

Since cocky was an egg
Long time ago
Silly as a two bob watch
Act crazy
Sink a few
Drink beer
Sink the boot in
Attack verbally and unfairly
Sink the slipper
Kick when fighting
Sitting on an ants' nest
In a situation that is about to get worse
Sitting up like Jacky
Conspicuously paying attention
Six of one and half a dozen of the other
Two things are almost the same/equal
Skew-whiff
Gone wrong; Untidy
Skinny as a sapling with the bark scraped off
Very thin
Slag off at...
Speak contemptuously of someone/something
Slap bang in the middle
Exact; Correct
Slow as a wet week in a caravan
Painfully slow
Smack a blue
Get into trouble/fight
Small potatoes
Small amount of money; Inexpensive
Smell bacon
See the police
Smell of an oily rag
Economical

Smokes him like a bad cigar
Beat his man and score a goal (football)

Snot someone
Punch/bash someone

So low he could parachute out of the belly of a snake
A person with no morals; Not trustworthy

So mean he wouldn't even let his dog drink from a mirage
Very mean and stingy; Will not spend money

So thin she wouldn't cast a shadow
Extremely thin female

So tight that he wouldn't shout if a shark bit him
Mean person who will not buy a round of beers

Soup strainer
Moustache

Southerly buster
Strong southerly winds

Space cadet
Not very clever person

Spag bol
Spaghetti Bolognese

Spend a penny
Go to the bathroom/toilet

Spinning a yarn
Telling a story for amusement

Splash the boots
Urinate (male)

Spitting chips
Angry; Upset

Spot on
Exact; Correct
Spray the bowl
Suffer from diarrhoea
Spread like wild fire
Spreads rapidly
Square eyes
Someone who watches too much television
Square up
Set things right; Pay the account
Stack on a blue
Become extremely angry; Fight
Stack your drapery
Put your coat on the ground before a fight
Stairway to heaven
Ladder in a lady's stocking
Standing around like an extra guest at a knock shop wedding
Standing around uselessly; Irritation/delay
Standing like a bandicoot on a burnt ridge
Feeling lonely and vulnerable
Stands out like a black crow in a bucket of milk
Obvious
Stands out like a country dunny
Immediately obvious
Stick in the mud
Boring unadventurous person
Stick your bib in
Interfering without being asked
Sticks out like dog's balls
Blatantly obvious
Stiff cheddar
Tough luck

Stir the possum
Create problems; Argue

Stole my thunder
Takes credit for something you did

Stones throw away
Short distance

Stone the crows!
Exclamation

Stop dragging the chain
Procrastinate; Hold up progress

Strapped for cash
Does not have much money

Strewth, cop a geek at that!
Look!

Stroppy lorikeet parade
Peak-hour traffic

Suck it and see
Try something that you have not done before to discover what it is like or whether it will be successful

Suss it out
Find the information

Sweating like a pregnant nun at confession
Nervous

Sweet Fanny Adams
Nothing

Sydney or the bush
All out effort regardless of the consequences if unsuccessful

T

Take a chill pill

Dismissive of someone who is agitated

Take a hike

Go away

Take a piece out of

Berate someone

Take a powder

Hurry away

Take a punt

Take a chance

Take a shine to

Like someone

Take by storm

Conquer someone/something in a fury

Take the biscuit/cake

Out-does everything else; Cannot be bettered

Take the bull by the horns

Confront a problem and deal with it openly

Take the mickey/piss out of...

Tease/ridicule someone

Talk the lid off an iron pot/hind leg off a donkey

Talks a lot

Talk under wet cement with a mouthful of marbles

Will not stop talking in a boring way

Talk you blind

Will not stop talking

Teeth to tail ration

Active personnel to administration

Tell someone who cares

Does not want to listen

That's the way the cookie/Violet Crumbles
Observation on the way things have turned out
That's a cracker
Not funny
That's about as funny as a kick in the head
Not funny
The good oil
Good news
Horse as bolted
Too late to do anything
The middle of the bloody day and not a bone in the truck
Achieved nothing, despite trying
There are two sides to every coin
There are different ways to think/do something
They've split the blanket
Couple have separated
Thick as a brick/two planks
Unintelligent
Thick ear
Injury from fighting
Things are crook in Tallarook
Things are going wrong
Think outside the square/box
New approach
Thinks her/his feet don't smell
Believes she/he is high class
Thinks his/her shit don't stink, but his/her farts give him away
Thinks he/she knows everything, but makes mistakes
Thinks the sun shines out of his/her arse
High regard for self; Snob
Thirty-seven degrees in the water bag
Hot day
Three parts gone
Almost drunk

Throw a spanner in the works
Unexpected problem
Throw the toys out of the pram
Loose one's temper/patience
Tickled pink
Very pleased
Tickle the till
Employee robs boss
Tide's gone out
Glass needs a refill
Tighter than a fish's bumhole
Miser
Toe jam
Lint/residue of body oil, sweat and dirt between toes
Touchy as a taipan
Temperamental and unpredictable
Tough as fencing wire
Very tough
Tough titties
Bad luck
Trap for young players
Problem for novices/the unaware
Tumble off the twig
Die
Turn it up
Expression of disbelief
Turn up for the books
Surprise ending
Twenty to the dozen
Doing something very fast
Two bobs worth
Opinion; Point of view
Two men and a dog
Poor attendance; Very few people

U

Under the affluence of inkahol
Drunk

Underground mutton
Rabbit

Until hell freezes over
Never

Up and down like a bride's nightie
Referring to something that fluctuates

Up and down like a yoyo
Things are in a mess

Up shit creek with only a fork to paddle with
In serious trouble

Up there Cazaly!
Call of encouragement (AFL)

Useful as an ashtray on a motorbike/flywire door on a submarine
Useless

Vague out
Not paying attention

Verandah above the toyshop/toolshed
Large belly on a man

Verbal diarrhoea
Can't stop talking

W

Waiting 'til the cows come home
Waiting all day/long time
Wagging school
Playing truant
Wake up Australia
A daydreamer
Walking papers
Dismissal from work
Waltzing Matilda
Wandering aimlessly around
Wanna have a go, do ya?
Do you want to fight/argue?
Wanna have a shot at the title, do ya champ?
Do you want to fight?
Do you want to try and do it?

Was your father a glass maker?
A person blocks your view
Weak as a wet whistle/piss
Very weak
Wear a smile
Be brave
Well turned out
Dressed well
Went through like a dose of salts
Leave quickly
Were you born in a tent/paddock with the slip rails down?
A person leaves door open
Wet arse and no fish
An ineffective task

Wet enough to bog a duck
Rained a lot
Wet oneself
Laugh hard
What a load of old cobblers
Load of nonsense
What and your shit don't stink?
A person thinks he/she is perfect
What are ya, a doctor?
A person gives you advice about your illness
What are you flapping your gums about now?
What are you talking about?
What do you do for a crust?
How do you earn your living?
What do you think this is, bush week?
Do you think I'm stupid?
What gives?
Please explain?
What's the John Dory?
What's the story? What is happening?

What's the strength?
What's wrong with that person?
What's your beef?
Why are you upset?
What's your song King Kong?
How do you feel?
When the crow/eagle shits
Pay day
When the shit hits the fan
A problem occurs
Where the crow flies backwards
Place a long way away
Whole box and dice
Everything

Whole kit and caboodle
Everything
Who's driving this bus?
Stop interfering
Who opened their lunch?
Who farted?
Who's robbing this coach?
Stop interfering; Don't tell me what to do
Why keep a dog and bark yourself?
Why do something when you can get someone else to do it for you?
Willy nilly
Disorder
With me?
Do you understand?
Without any shadow of a doubt
It is a fact
Won't have a bar of...
Rejects
Woolloomooloo uppercut
Kick to the groin
Worm your way out of it
Try to get out of doing something
Would bet on two flies walking up the wall
Compulsive gambler
Would knock your socks off
Something amazing
Wouldn't be dead for quids
Having fun; Enjoying life
Wouldn't give you the time of day
An uncooperative person
Wouldn't go two rounds with a revolving door
Weak; Incompetent

Wouldn't have a bar of it

Inability to tolerate an action/situation

Wouldn't have the foggest

Do not know

Wouldn't it rot your socks off

Something annoying/disgusting

Wouldn't know if a tram was up him unless the conductor rang the bell

Person does not think about the future

Wouldn't know if his arse was on fire

Ignorant

Wouldn't know him if I found him in my Cornflakes packet

Complete stranger

Wouldn't piss on him if he was on fire

Statement of contempt

Wouldn't read about it

Unusual; Unfortunate

Wouldn't shout in a shark attack

Unhelpful; Not buy a round of drinks

Wouldn't touch with a ten-foot pole

Have nothing to do with it

Wouldn't use him/her for shark bait

Hold someone in very low regard

Wouldn't work in an iron lung

Lazy individual

Would put a smile on your face

Make you happy

Would talk a glass eye to sleep

Boring person

Wreck something

Break/spoil/sabotage/destroy something

Write off

Something, usually a car that costs too much to fix

Y

Ya telling me

Agreeing with something

Yanking my chain

Mislead; Lie

You are off the rails

Behaving in a way that is not acceptable to society

Your blood's worth bottling

Did something excellent; Worth praising

You can't walk on one leg!

Yes, thanks, I will!

You don't have to be dead to be stiff

Run of bad luck for no reason

You'd want to know the ins and outs of a magpie's arsehole

Answer to an inquisitive person

You look like a stunned mullet

Surprised

You look like something the cat dragged in

Dirty, Untidy appearance

You must be the world's only living brain donor

Stupid to the extreme

You're a gunna

All talk and no action

You're as good as two blondes put together

Not very smart

Your goose is cooked

You are in trouble

Your shout

Your turn to buy the drinks

You tell him, I stutter
Sick and tired of trying to explain
You've got to be in it to win it
Buy a ticket
You've got buckleys, mate
No chance
You've got two chances, buckleys and none
Impossible

British English hand-me-downs & Aussie rhyming slang

Many of these terms originated from the convicts, who were deported from the United Kingdom. Over time they have been given an Aussie twist.

Adam and Eve	believe
After darks	sharks
Al Capone	phone
Almond rocks	socks
Apples and pears	stairs
Babbling brook	cook (wife)
Bag of fruit	suit
Ballarat	hat
Barney Rubble	trouble
Barry Crocker	shocker
Big 'n' bub	pub
Billy lids	kids
Blood blister	sister
Boat race	face
Bob Hope	soap
Bowl of fruit	suit
Bowler hat	cat
Brass tacks	facts
Brave and bold	cold
Bread and honey	money
Bread and jam	tram
Britney Spears	beers
Brown bread	dead
Bugs Bunny	money
Bull and cow	row

Butcher's hook	look
Canoes	shoes
Captain Cook	look
Cat's hiss	piss
Charlie Wheeler	Sheila (woman)
Cheese and kisses	missus; wife; girlfriend
Cherry plum	mum
Chewy toffee	coffee
China plate	mate
Christmas crackered	knackered (exhausted)
Cloud seven	heaven
Comic guts	stomach
Country cousin	dozen
Crust of bread	head
Currency lad or lass	a native born Australian
Curry and rice	price
Dad 'n' Dave	shave
Daisy roots	boots
Dander	anger
Dead horse	sauce (tomato)
Dalai Lamas	dramas
Dickie bird	word
Dickie dirt	shirt
Dickory dock	clock
Dig in the grave	shave
Ding dong	sing song
Dodge and shirk	work
Dog and bone	phone
Dog's eye	meat pie
Dog's eye and dead horse	pie and sauce
Donald Duck	luck
Donkey vote	stupid vote
Dry rots	trots (diarrhoea)

Ducks and drakes	shakes
Ducks and geese	police
Duke of Cork	talk
Dunlop tyre	liar
Dunny budgie	blowfly
Dustbin lids	kids
Eau de cologne	telephone
Elephant's trunk	drunk
Esky lid	derogatory term for a bodyguard
Fairy bower	shower
Farmer Giles	piles; haemorrhoids
Forgive and forget	cigarette
Frog and toad	road
Froth and bubble	trouble
Full bottle	knowledgeable, an expert
Gary Abblett	tablet
Gary Glitter	bitter (beer)
Gay and hearty	party
German band	hand
Gin sling	ring (phone)
Ginger Meggs	legs
Give someone gip	to annoy someone
Go for a Burton	to be missing
Goose's neck	cheque
Greens	wages
Gregory Peck	cheque
Grim and gory	story
Grin and chronic	gin and tonic
Half inch	pinch (steal)
Ham and eggs	legs
Hammer and tack	back
Hamstead heath	teeth
Hard hit	shit

Harold bolt	run away
Have a Captains Cook	have a look
Hit and miss	kiss
Hit the frog and toad	go down the road
Hollow log	dog
Holy ghost	toast
Horse and cart	fart
Irish jig	wig
I suppose	nose
Jack and Jill	bill
Jack Jones	alone
Jam jar	car
Jam tart	heart
Jimmy Dancer	cancer
Joe Blake	snake
Joe soap	dope (stupid person)
John Dory	story
John Hopper	copper (policeman)
Johnny Horner	corner
Johnny Raper	paper
Kitchen sink	drink
Lemon lime	good time
Lemon squash	wash
Loaf of bread	use your head
Look-the-loop	soup
Mal Meningas	fingers
Malcolm Bright	light
Marbles and conkers	bonkers (mad)
Mars bar	car
Mickey Mouse	grouse (great)
Mince pies	eyes
Moby Dick	sick
Molly the monk	drunk

Monkies' arses	glasses
Mother's ruin	gin
Mud pies	eyes
Mutt and Jeff	deaf
Mystery bags	snags (sausages)
Nails and screws	news
Near and far	bar
Ned Kelly	belly
Noah's ark	shark
Norman von Nida	spider
North and south	mouth
Now is the hour	shower
No wucking furries	no worries
Nutmeg	leg
Oily rag	fag (cigarette)
Old Ned	bed
Oliver Twist	pissed (drunk)
On the beak	stink
On the floor	poor
On the Murray cod	on the nod/credit
Optic nerve	perve (look)
Oxford scholar	dollar
Pat Malone	alone
Paul Keating	meeting
Pen and ink	stink
Peter Mertens	curtains
Piccadilly	chilly
Pig's arse	glass
Pig's ear	beer
Plates of meat	feet
Pipe your eye	cry
Porky pie	lie
Pot of good cheer	beer

Rabbit and pork	talk
Radio rental	mental
Raspberry tart	fart
Razzmatazz	jazz (excitement)
Red hot	pot of beer
Red hots	trots (horse-racing/diarrhoea)
Reg Grundies	undies (underwear)
Rhodes scholar	dollar
Rhythm 'n' blues	shoes
Rifle range	change
Rock and lurch	church
Rock 'n' Roll	dole
Rocky Ed	head
Rod Laver	favour
Rosie Lee	tea
Rubbity-dub	pub
Ruby Murray	curry
Saint Louis Blues	shoes
Sandy McNab	cab
Sausage and mash	cash
Septic tank	yank
Skin and blister	sister
Sky rocket	pocket
Smash and grab	cab
Snag sanga	sausage sandwich
Soda roll	goal
Soldier's bold	cold
Squiz/squizzy	look at
Steak and kidney	Sydney
Sticky beak	peek (look)
Stiff shitty	city
Stock and die	pie
Sweeney Todd	Flying Squad (police)

Tea leaf	thief
This and that	hat
Tiddly wink	drink
Tin lids	kids
Tit for tat (titfer)	hat
To and from	pom (English person)
Toby jugs	lugs (ears)
Todd Sloan	alone
Tom and Dick	sick
Tom Tit	shit
Trick cyclist	psychiatrist
Trams and trains	brains; drains
Trouble and strife	wife
Turkish bath	laugh
Uncle Dick	sick
Uncle Willy	silly
Vera Lynn	gin
Wally Grout	shout
Warwick Farm	arm
Weasel and stoat	coat
Whistle and flute	suit
Wooden pegs	legs
You beaut	ute
Young and frisky	whisky
Young and old	cold
Zane Grey	pay